Abortion and the
Conscience
of the Nation

Abortion and the Conscience of the Nation

Ronald Reagan

NRP

New Regency Publishing
Sacramento, California

www.nrpub.com

ISBN 0-9641125-3-1

Cover art and interior layout by
Jeff Evans / JC Evans Communications
www.jc-evans.com

New Regency Publishing

1 (800) BOOK; NEW
1 (800) 266-5639

printed in Canada

CONTENTS

FOREWORD

RONALD REAGAN, LIFEGUARD

By the Honorable William P. Clark,
former U.S. Secretary of the Interior*

President Reagan's record of public service reveals throughout that no moral issue was of greater importance to him than the dignity and sanctity of all

---

*Editor's Note: According to Edmund Morris, official biographer of U.S. President Ronald Reagan, Judge Clark is "the most important and influential person in the first [Reagan] administration, and in fact the only person in the entire two terms who had any kind of spiritual intimacy with the President."

human life. His beliefs were established early in life, in the spiritual environment inspired by his devoted and devout mother Nelle, with the backing of Jack Reagan, his fiercely humanitarian father.

The value of each person's life as well as the power of one man's actions were further established during his college summertime employment as a lifeguard in Dixon, Illinois. In just two summers of service at Lowell Beach, young Ronald saved more than seventy swimmers from drowning.

As a young adult, Reagan's convictions were tragically reinforced by the loss of his daughter Christina, only three days into her life – this, at a time Reagan himself was fighting for his own life, in another hospital, against viral pneumonia.

Those of us who entered political life with Ronald Reagan in the 1960s, when he was elected Governor of California, found him predictable in his decisions, as these actions were so firmly rooted in his beliefs. He was never persuaded by – and at times did not even wish to hear – the results of political polls. He would counsel, "Let's do the right thing, and the good politics will follow," as well as "We can accomplish almost anything together, if we do not concern ourselves with the question of who might receive the credit." While this might well account for the slow pace of historians in rendering him the credit he is rightly due, it won him our lasting admiration.

Perhaps his greatest disappointment in public life occurred in his first year of office. As the new California Governor, he was confronted by one piece of legislation which proposed liberalizing access to legal abortion. By a lopsided majority, the bill raced through the legislature, following the lead of other "progressive" states. Members of his staff had pointed out that the veto he planned would be overridden by the commanding majority of the opposition party in the state legislature. The Governor went into semi-seclusion for a long weekend. There he studied the moral, legal, and medical aspects of abortion, and the extensive reach of the other life issues. He later emerged, saying, "When this subject arises again, we shall be prepared." And he certainly was, as the future proved. No political leader in American history has spoken out more forcefully and more frequently for the dignity of all human life than Ronald Reagan.

While he often challenged the words and actions of his political adversaries, I cannot recall an unkind word that the President uttered against another person. I cannot think of any personal attack he ever made on anyone in the many years I worked with him, again, out of respect for each human being.

"The real question today," he would say, "is not when human life begins, but what is the true value and meaning of human life." And in his

*President Reagan
with Judge Clark*

famous March 1983 "Evil Empire" speech, which most remember simply as an indictment of Communist Russia, he actually inveighed against all government which denigrates the value of innocent human life:

> More than a decade ago, a Supreme Court decision literally wiped off the books of 50 states statutes protecting the rights of innocent unborn children. Abortion on demand now takes the lives of up to one and a half million unborn children a year. Human life legislation ending this tragedy will some day pass the Congress and you and I must never rest until it does. Unless and until it can be proven the unborn child is not a living person, then its right to life, liberty, and the pursuit of happiness must be protected.

You may remember that when abortion on demand began, many warned that the practice would lead to a decline in respect for all human life, and the philosophical premises used to justify abortion on demand would ultimately be used to justify other attacks on the sacredness of human life, including infanticide or mercy killing. Tragically enough, these warnings are proving all too true.

The President knew he had been given a spiritual mission – a special role in the Divine plan of life. He was deeply prayerful without public display, often using the words of Abraham Lincoln: "I am frequently forced to my knees in the overwhelming conviction that I have no place else to go."

Then came the assassination attempt in 1981,

considered by the President a wake-up call, driving him onward even more forcefully in his spiritual role. Thereafter, the world witnessed his increasing courage and action in the war of good against evil, the basis of his policy of peace through military and moral strength. Aggressively implemented, that policy led as he predicted to our shift from mutual assured destruction (MAD) to his nuclear zero option, to the destruction of the Berlin Wall and ultimately to the dissolution of the Soviet Empire. He also found time to produce the only book written by a sitting U.S. President, *Abortion and the Conscience of the Nation*, which follows his essay of the same title, first appearing in *Human Life Review*, Spring 1983.

I firmly believe that President Reagan, if informed today, would be gravely disappointed by the many people in both political parties who have attempted to walk away from this predominant human rights issue of his agenda, as they did from the similar issue of slavery a century and a half ago. Some contend that the life issue, like slavery, has been settled by the Court, or, acknowledging that abortion is an evil, have rationalized that it is a necessary evil. But evil it is, and the President felt the overriding obligation of his office was to cure this terrible wrong.

And I believe that the American public – which he frequently asserted is far wiser than the government – holds Ronald Reagan for what he truly is and will always be: a champion of all that is right and true and just; a firm believer and practitioner of all that makes America great; an advocate of the good; a defender of the innocent, young and old alike.

A fourth-generation Californian, William P. Clark attended Stanford University, served in the US Army Counter Intelligence Corps, and later attended Loyola University Law School in Los Angeles. After serving as chief of staff to Governor Ronald Reagan in California, he became Judge of the Superior Court, Justice of the California Court of Appeal, and finally Justice of the California Supreme Court before being called to Washington to serve under President Reagan as Deputy Secretary of State, National Security Adviser, and Secretary of the Interior.

Ronald Reagan,
Civilization's Advocate

By Brian Johnston,

Western Regional Director,
National Right To Life Committee

As a first generation American, with some regularity I return to Ireland, the land of my parents' birth. On a recent visit, I had the opportunity to spend time with a fellow American and dear friend, Judge William Clark. I have had the good pleasure of making Judge Clark's acquaintance, and developing a warm friendship through his involvement and interest in the Right to Life cause and my work with the National Right to Life Committee. While our free-ranging conversation that evening touched on matters from Irish art and politics, to California history, to life in today's Austria; our discussion returned again and again to a speech made by President Ronald Reagan early in his first administration. That speech is known today as the "Evil Empire" speech; it is considered by many the most provocative of any made by President Reagan, or by any recent President.

I have long been a Reagan fan, but that evening Judge Clark illuminated for me the elegant beauty of that speech and how it encapsulated President Reagan's worldview. It is clear that Ronald Reagan understood much more than mere politics and effective communication. Ronald Reagan understood the appropriate role of the vast power and authority in his hands. He understood what lies at the very heart of civilization, that it could be lost, and that it must be defended.

Edmund Morris, President Reagan's official biographer, has called Judge Clark the man spiritually closest to Ronald Reagan. That evening in Ireland he told me that the "Evil Empire " speech in many ways summed up the heart of Ronald Reagan's political philosophy. "Few people have taken the time to examine the context of that speech," said Judge Clark. Its theme was not simply the evils of communism, but more to the point of our immediate, mutual concern, "Its true theme was the value of every individual human life." It was, simply put, a Right-to-Life speech. The President began by citing America's historical commitment to God, decrying the flawed logic of *Roe v. Wade*, and mourning the millions of lives needlessly lost. He explained why the *Baby Doe* regulations were needed to protect handicapped infants from infanticide. He prophesied the coming lure of euthanasia. America, "the last, best hope of man ... was seeing ... a prevailing attitude of modern day secularism, discarding the tried and time tested

values upon which our civilization is based."
At this point the President departed from the prepared text. He slipped in two paragraphs that would change history, words which had not been vetted with his more pragmatic advisors. "There is sin and evil in the world." Marxist-Leninism and specifically the Soviet Union, "which holds the omnipotence of the state over the lives of individual men," was the focus of this modern evil, "...it is an evil empire." It was a sentiment that Reagan had felt with all his heart, but historians now tell us that U.S. diplomats and advisors had urged the President to never use such terms. As Frank Warner of the Associated Press put it, the "Evil Empire speech disturbed the political universe... it set off a global chain reaction that led to the fall of the Berlin Wall, and Soviet Communism itself." (Copies of the "Evil Empire" speech of 3/08/83 are available through the Reagan Library, e-mail: library@reagan.nara.gov)

Many Reagan detractors have dismissed him as

Courtesy Ronald Reagan Library

"a simple jingoist," and the speech as "typical saber-rattling." Many opponents and even some supporters view him as, at heart, simply an anti-communist, or an advocate of less government, or a libertarian, or an economic "supply-sider." But I would venture that these are mere surface facets of his policies, and that the Ronald Reagan "worldview" has much more in common with the great philosophers and the timeless principles of all sound government. After hearing Judge Clark's observations, and re-reading the speech itself, it appears to me that in the "Evil Empire" speech (as in many of his other speeches) Ronald Reagan essentially asserted that the definitive standard of ALL governments is how well they protect the lives of their own innocent citizens.

Ronald Reagan stands amidst a pantheon of great, and often misunderstood statesmen who asserted the deceivingly simple premise of the "right to life." Jefferson, Madison, and their colleagues understood more than just that, "government derives its authority from the consent of the governed." Government therefore ensures its proper place only in as much as it protects the actual *lives* and rights of the governed, in particular the innocent. The self-evident fact to America's founders was that the most precious and pre-eminent of all rights was the right to live. *"The care of human life and happiness,"* Jefferson wrote in 1809, *"and not their destruction, is the first and only legitimate object of good government."*

Some 'supply-side' economists of today applaud as Reagan's finest virtue his embrace of Adam Smith's "invisible hand." This is Smith's theory of market forces as outlined in the Scot's famous work, Wealth of Nations. I am often surprised however, when I find that relatively few 'supply-side' Smith fans are aware of his preceding work, The Theory of Moral Sentiments. This he wrote as the necessary predicate for his conclusions in Wealth of Nations. Smith asserted, *"The most sacred laws of justice are the laws which guard the life and person of our neighbor."* What is the ownership of private property if one is not first assured of the right to simply live?

If some doubt that President Reagan held as his benchmark the "right to life" ideal – that the true measure of any civilized government is whether it protects the lives of its innocent – they need only read his accompanying essay. It is very clear however, that this is not just a passing, personal pique. The most significant trial of Ronald Reagan's lifetime was decided on this very topic, and was international in scope. This trial took place in Nuremberg, Germany in 1947.

Contrary to simplistic revisionist history, the Nuremberg Trials did *not* try Nazi war leaders. German generals and civil authorities were not tried for "starting the war," or invading Poland, or France, or the Sudetenland. At Nuremberg, German civilians were tried, and punished, for their treatment of other German civilians. In what was at that time the most technologically advanced nation in civilization, minor civil authorities were judged to have acted barbarically. This was not because they slaughtered citizens of nations opposed – but quite simply because they oversaw and orchestrated the slaughter of their own vulnerable citizens.

Judge Clark's comments to me that evening

outside Dublin have since allowed me to see so much more in the other speeches of President Reagan, and to see so much more of President Reagan's 'standard' at work in the events of history. Many historians have compared Reagan to Cato the Elder of Rome. The "cold-warrior" of his day, Cato closed every speech with the invective, *"Carthago delenda est!"* *"Carthage (the opposing superpower of the day) must be destroyed!"* Cato was an outspoken advocate of Rome's Old Republic. A social conservative, among other things he was committed to the primacy of the family as the essential cultural unit.

Many historians point out that Cato insightfully understood that only one culture and civilization could rule the Mediterranean and eventually the world. And though he did not live to see it himself, Carthage, Cato's "evil empire," was in fact utterly destroyed. The legionnaires' orders were that not one of the city's stones be left standing on another. To ensure no rekindling of a future Carthaginian culture, the denuded fields were then sown with salt. The near-nuclear devastation reminded some historians of the potentially vast destructive power at President Reagan's disposal as he resisted the evils of the Soviet empire.

But relatively few historians have emphasized a deeper motivation in Cato's resolve, the preservation of Civilization itself, and his resistance to institutionalized barbarism. Will Durant in The Story of Civilization retells this scene likely witnessed by Cato in his early tour of Carthage – it is a scene of routine human sacrifice as a civil duty.

> [Living children] were placed on the outstretched and inclined arms of the idol and rolled off into the fire beneath; their cries were drowned in the noise of trumpets and cymbals; their mothers were required to look upon the scene without

moan or tear, lest they be accused of impiety and lose the credit due them. (*Story of Civilization, vol. 1, pg. 60.*)

The actual sacrifice of one's own child in the hope that it might bring future peace and prosperity is clearly not a new idea. President Reagan may not have been aware of the fact, but at the time of his own "Evil Empire" speech, Russian women were routinely sacrificing their children having an average of eight abortions each. However, he was clearly aware of the connection between abortion, the destruction of innocent human life, and the evils reflected in Communism.

In the spring of 2000, *The American Experience*, a PBS TV program, presented a biography of Ronald Reagan. Judge Clark's assertion of Reagan's true motives in resisting Russian communism, and the right to life context of the "Evil Empire" speech, were of course not presented. But as PBS closed the Reagan years it showed excerpts of a speech made by him in Moscow in 1988, the last year of his final term. Gorbachev was using *détente, glasnost,* and *perestroika* as window-dressing to beautify a flawed regime.

Reagan was about to meet Gorbachev at the Kremlin for further peace talks, but again he eluded his pragmatic handlers. Summoning Russian dissidents to the American Embassy for breakfast, the American President reminded them of why he would be unrelenting in facing down the Soviet leadership. The hair rose on my neck as the persecuted dissidents cheered Reagan's proclamation of his most basic of all principles, *"On the fundamental dignity of the human person,"* the President boomed out – jaw set and eyes aflame – *"there can be no relenting!"*

Ronald Reagan's resolution to assert the protection of the innocent individual as the definitive moral guide for not only his own nation – but for all nations – makes him more than simply an advocate of America and Americanism. He was his era's boldest advocate of Civilization itself, and its greatest protector. His assertion of these fundamental rights and the preeminence of the right to life will, I believe, eventually gain him history's enduring recognition as a statesman.

———

Brian Johnston is the Western Regional Director of the National Right to Life Committee. He has served as California Commissioner on Aging, on California's Board of Examiners of Nursing Homes, on the state's Elder Abuse Task Force, and on the board of directors of the National Legal Center for the Medically Dependent and Disabled. He is author of the book, DEATH AS A SALESMAN; WHAT'S WRONG WITH ASSISTED SUICIDE.

INTRODUCTION

THE PRO-LIFE LEGACY OF
PRESIDENT RONALD REAGAN

By Wanda Franz, Ph.D.

President, National Right to Life Committee

Ronald Reagan was a great president. He was a great statesman and leader. And he demonstrated that greatness in the dignity with which he carried himself, the respect for the office he held, and the courage with which he made difficult decisions. He brought to the presidency his great love for America and his ability to demonstrate that love in his own life and in his actions as president.

He loved America because it stands for freedom and equality before the law for everyone. And Reagan understood that freedom and equality before the law are based on a more fundamental principle: the intrinsic, God-given dignity and value of each human person. Without this fundamental principle, this "endowment by the Creator," the invocation in the Declaration of Independence of "the unalienable right to life, liberty and the pursuit of happiness" would be a hollow statement, a noble sentiment of little consequence.

Ronald Reagan understood this great truth and acted on it. Thus he had compassion and respect for each human person regardless of age, disability, race or social class. What his essay expresses in words was matched by deeds in his presidency.

The Reagan legacy includes a wide range of pro-life actions—actions that defied the pro-abortion culture and often had to be pursued over the objections of a hostile leadership in Congress. He worked to pass the "Baby Doe" regulations to protect newborn children with disabilities when they are threatened by denial of nutrition, medically indicated treatment, or even general care. He instituted policies prohibiting funding for experimentation on unborn children. He established the "Mexico City" policy under which private organizations, which perform or actively promote abortion as a method of family planning in other nations, are ineligible for funds under the "population assistance" program. He supported congressional efforts to limit funding of abortions. He worked to enforce congressional directives to prevent so-called "family planning" programs from advocating abortion as a means of birth control as part of Title X. President Reagan also submitted to Congress the "President's Pro-Life Bill of 1987," that would have put Congress on record against *Roe v. Wade*, permanently prohibited federal funding of abortion, and denied Title 10 "family planning" funds to organizations which perform or refer for abortions.

President Reagan openly supported efforts to reverse *Roe v. Wade*. He supported the pro-life plank in the Republican Platform and used every opportunity to express his support for the right to life. His leadership helped galvanize the pro-life movement into the powerful force that it is today. At the National Right to Life Committee, we are proud to have worked with President Reagan to uphold and reaffirm the fundamental principles that undergird our Democracy.

At the Annual Proudly Pro-Life Dinner in 1997, the National Right to Life Committee recognized President Reagan with a special tribute for his leadership in promoting pro-life initiatives.

Regrettably, since President Reagan left office, *Roe v. Wade* has been reaffirmed and expanded by *Planned Parenthood of Southeastern Pennsylvania v. Casey* and *Stenberg v. Carhart*. Yet he has taught us to persevere in the face of difficulties because our cause is just. In the end, *Roe v. Wade* and its progeny will be reversed and, in spite of all temporary setbacks, the "unalienable right to life" that is "endowed by the Creator" will be restored.

The words expressed in Reagan's essay are as vital and relevant today as when they were first written. The pro-life movement will always be indebted to President Ronald Reagan for his word and deed. As his presidency showed, respecting the God-given rights of every individual person is one of the necessary conditions for greatness.

———

Wanda Franz, Ph.D. is the president of the National Right to Life Committee, and host of the daily radio program, Pro-Life Perspective. She is the author of numerous articles and of a college textbook on early child development. Dr. Franz has lectured throughout the world, and made a forceful presentation at the United Nations Conference on Population in 1994. She is a developmental psychologist and professor of Child Development at West Virginia University.

ABORTION AND THE CONSCIENCE
OF THE NATION

By President Ronald Reagan

The tenth anniversary of the Supreme Court decision in *Roe v. Wade* is a good time for us to pause and reflect.* Our nationwide policy of abortion-on-demand through all nine months of pregnancy was neither voted for by our people nor enacted by our legislators – not a single state had such unrestricted abortion before the Supreme Court decreed it to be national policy in 1973. But the consequences of this judicial decision are now

* This essay originally appeared in 1983.

obvious: since 1973, more than 15 million
unborn children have had their lives snuffed
out by legalized abortions. That is over ten
times the number of Americans lost in all our
nation's wars.

Make no mistake, abortion-on-demand is not a
right granted by the Constitution. No serious
scholar, including one disposed to agree
with the Court's result, has argued that the
framers of the Constitution intended to create
such a right. Shortly after the *Roe v. Wade*
decision, Professor John Hart Ely, now
Dean of Stanford Law School, wrote that the
opinion "is not constitutional law and
gives almost no sense of an obligation to try to
be." Nowhere do the plain words of the
Constitution even hint at a "right" so
sweeping as to permit abortion up to the time
the child is ready to be born. Yet that is what
the Court ruled.

As an act of "raw judicial power" (to use Justice White's biting phrase), the decision by the seven-man majority in *Roe v. Wade* has so far been made to stick. But the Court's decision has by no means settled the debate. Instead, *Roe v. Wade* has become a continuing prod to the conscience of the nation.

Abortion concerns not just the unborn child, it concerns every one of us. The English poet, John Donne, wrote: "...any man's death diminishes me, because I am involved in mankind; and therefore never send to know for whom the bell tolls; it tolls for thee."

We cannot diminish the value of one category of human life – the unborn – without diminishing the value of all human life. We saw tragic proof of this truism last year when the Indiana courts allowed the starvation death of "Baby Doe" in Bloomington because the child had Down's Syndrome.

Many of our fellow citizens grieve over the loss of life that has followed *Roe v. Wade.* Margaret Heckler, soon after being nominated to head the largest department of our government, Health and Human Services, told an audience that she believed abortion to be the greatest moral crisis facing our country today. And the revered Mother Teresa, who works in the streets of Calcutta ministering to dying people in her world famous mission of mercy, has said that "the greatest misery of our time is the generalized abortion of children."

Over the first two years of my administration I have closely followed and assisted efforts in Congress to reverse the tide of abortion – efforts of congressmen, senators and citizens respond-ing to an urgent moral crisis. Regrettably, I have also seen the massive efforts of those who, under the banner of "freedom of choice," have so far blocked every effort to reverse nationwide abortion-on-demand.

Despite the formidable obstacles before us, we must not lose heart. This is not the first time our country has been divided by a Supreme Court decision that denied the value of certain human lives. The *Dred Scott* decision of 1857 was not overturned in a day, or a year, or even a decade. At first, only a minority of Americans recognized and deplored the moral crisis brought about by denying the full humanity of our black brothers and sisters; but that minority persisted in their vision and finally prevailed. They did it by appealing to the hearts and minds of their countrymen, to the truth of human dignity under God. From their example, we know that respect for the sacred value of human life is too deeply engrained in the hearts of our people to remain forever suppressed. But the great majority of the American people have not yet made their voices heard, and we cannot expect them to, any more than the public voice arose against slavery *until* the issue is clearly framed and presented.

What then, is the real issue? I have often said that when we talk about abortion, we are talking about two lives – the life of the mother and the life of the unborn child. Why else do we call a pregnant woman a mother? I have also said that anyone who doesn't feel sure whether we are talking about a second human life should clearly give life the benefit of the doubt. If you don't know whether a body is alive or dead, you would never bury it. I think this consideration itself should be enough for all of us to insist on protecting the unborn.

The case against abortion does not rest here, however, for medical practice confirms at every step the correctness of these moral sensibilities. Modern medicine treats the unborn child as a patient. Medical pioneers have made great breakthroughs in treating the unborn – for genetic problems, vitamin deficiencies, irregular heart rhythms, and other medical conditions. Who can forget George Will's moving account of the little boy who underwent brain surgery six times during the nine weeks before he was born? Who is the *patient* if not that tiny unborn human being who can feel pain when he or she is approached by doctors who come to kill rather than to cure?

The real question today is not when human life begins, but, *what is the value of human life?* The abortionist who reassembles the arms and legs of a tiny baby to make sure all its parts have been torn from its mother's body can hardly doubt whether it is a human being. The real question for him and for all of us is whether that tiny human life has a God-given right to be protected by the law – the same right we have.

What more dramatic confirmation could we have of the real issue than the Baby Doe case in Bloomington, Indiana? The death of that tiny infant tore at the hearts of all Americans because the child was undeniably a live human being –

President Reagan

Courtesy Ronald Reagan Library

one lying helpless before the eyes of the doctors and the eyes of the nation. The real issue for the courts was *not* whether Baby Doe was a human being. The real issue was whether to protect the life of a human being who had Down's Syndrome, who would probably be mentally handicapped, but who needed a routine surgical procedure to unblock his esophagus and allow him to eat. A doctor testified to the presiding judge that, even with his physical problem corrected, Baby Doe would have a "non-existent" possibility for "a minimally adequate quality of life" – in other words, that retardation was the equivalent of a crime deserving the death penalty. The judge let Baby Doe starve and die, and the Indiana Supreme Court sanctioned his decision.

Federal law does not allow federally assisted hospitals to decide that Down's Syndrome infants are not worth treating, much less to decide to starve them to death. Accordingly, I have directed the Departments of Justice and Health and Human Services to apply civil rights regulations to protect handicapped newborns. All hospitals receiving federal funds must post notices which will clearly state that failure to feed handicapped babies is prohibited by federal law. The basic issue is whether to value and protect the lives of the handicapped, whether to recognize the sanctity of human life. This is the same basic issue that underlies the question of abortion.

The 1981 Senate hearings on the beginning of human life brought out the basic issue more clearly than ever before. The main medical and scientific witnesses who testified disagreed on many things, but not on the *scientific* evidence that the unborn child is alive, is a distinct individual, or is a member of the human species. They did disagree over the *value* question, whether to give value to a human life at its early and most vulnerable stages of existence.

Regrettably, we live at a time when some persons do *not* value all human life. They want to pick and choose which individuals have value. Some have said that only those individuals with "consciousness of self" are human beings. One such writer has followed this deadly logic and concluded that "shocking as it may seem, a newly born infant is not a human being."

A Nobel Prize winning scientist has suggested that if a handicapped child "were not declared fully human until three days after birth, then all parents could be allowed the choice." In other words, "quality control" to see if newly born human beings are up to snuff.

Obviously, some influential people want to deny that every human life has intrinsic, sacred worth. They insist that a member of the human race must have certain qualities before they accord him or her status as a "human being."

Events have borne out the editorial in a California medical journal which explained three years before *Roe v. Wade* that the social acceptance of abortion is a "defiance of the long-held Western ethic of intrinsic and equal value for every human life regardless of its stage, condition, or status."

Every legislator, every doctor, and every citizen needs to recognize that the real issue is whether to affirm and protect the sanctity of all human life, or to embrace a social ethic where some human lives are valued and others are not. As a nation, we must choose between the sanctity of life ethic and the "quality of life" ethic.

I have no trouble identifying the answer our nation has always given to this basic question, and the answer that I hope and pray it will give in the future. America was founded by men and women who shared a vision of the value of each and every individual. They stated this vision clearly from the very start in the Declaration of Independence, using words that every school-boy and schoolgirl can recite:

We hold these truths to be self-evident, that all men are created equal, that they are endowed by their Creator with certain un-alienable rights, that among these are life, liberty, and the pursuit of happiness.

We fought a terrible war to guarantee that one category of mankind – black people in America – could not be denied the inalienable rights with which their Creator endowed them. The great champion of the sanctity of all human life in that day, Abraham Lincoln, gave us his assessment of the Declaration's purpose. Speaking of the framers of that noble document, he said:

This was their majestic interpretation of the economy of the Universe. This was their lofty, and wise, and noble understanding of the justice of the Creator to His creatures. Yes, gentlemen, to all His creatures, to the whole great family of man. In their enlightened belief, nothing stamped with the divine image and likeness was sent into the world to be trodden on... They grasped not only the whole race of man then living, but they reached forward and seized upon the farthest posterity. They erected a beacon to guide their children and their children's children, and the countless myriads who should inhabit the earth in other ages.

He warned also of the danger we would face if we closed our eyes to the value of life in any category of human beings:

> I should like to know if taking this old Declaration of Independence, which declares that all men are equal upon principle and making exceptions to it where will it stop. If one man says it does not mean a Negro, why not another say it does not mean some other man?

When Congressman John A. Bingham of Ohio drafted the Fourteenth Amendment to guarantee the rights of life, liberty, and property to all human beings, he explained that *all* are "entitled to the protection of American law, because its divine spirit of equality declares that all men are created equal." He said the rights guaranteed by the amendment would therefore apply to "any human being." Justice William Brennan, in another case decided only the year before *Roe v. Wade,* referred to our society as one that "strongly affirms the sanctity of life."

Another William Brennan – not the Justice – has reminded us of the terrible consequences that can follow when a nation rejects the sanctity of life ethic:

> The cultural environment for a human holocaust is present whenever any society can be misled into defining individuals as less than human and therefore devoid of value and respect.

As a nation today, we have *not* rejected the sanctity of human life. The American people have not had an opportunity to express their view on the sanctity of human life in the unborn. I am convinced that Americans do not want to play God with the value of human life. It is not for us to decide who is worthy to live and who is not. Even the Supreme Court's opinion in *Roe v. Wade* did not explicitly reject the traditional American idea of intrinsic worth and value in all human life; it simply dodged this issue.

The Congress has before it several measures that would enable our people to reaffirm the sanctity of human life, even the smallest and the youngest and the most defenseless. The Human Life Bill expressly recognizes the unborn as human beings and accordingly protects them as persons under our Constitution. This bill, first introduced by Senator Jesse Helms, provided the vehicle for the Senate hearings in 1981 which contributed so much to our understanding of the real issue of abortion.

The Respect Human Life Act, just introduced in the ninety-eighth Congress, states in its first section that the policy of the United States is "to protect innocent life both before and after birth." This bill, sponsored by Congressman Henry Hyde and Senator Roger Jepsen, prohibits the federal government from performing abortions or assisting those who do so, except to save the life of the mother. It also addresses the pressing issue of infanticide which, as we have seen, flows inevitably from permissive abortion as another step in the denial of the inviolability of innocent human life.

I have endorsed each of these measures, as well as the more difficult route of constitutional amendment, and I will give these initiatives my full support. Each of them, in different ways, attempts to reverse the tragic policy of abortion-on-demand imposed by the Supreme Court ten years ago. Each of them is a decisive way to affirm the sanctity of human life.

We must all educate ourselves to the reality of the horrors taking place. Doctors today know that unborn children can feel a touch within the womb and that they respond to pain. But how many Americans are aware that abortion techniques are allowed today, in all fifty states, that burn the skin of a baby with a salt solution, in an agonizing death that can last for hours?

Another example: two years ago, the *Philadelphia Inquirer* ran a Sunday special supplement on "The Dreaded Complication." The "dreaded complication" referred to in the article – the complication feared by doctors who perform abortions – is the *survival of* the child despite all the painful attacks during the abortion procedure. Some unborn children *do* survive the late-term abortions the Supreme Court has made legal. Is there any question that these victims of abortion deserve our attention and protection? Is there any question that those who *don't* survive were living human beings before they were killed?

Late-term abortions, especially when the baby survives, but is then killed by starvation, neglect, or suffocation, show once again the link between abortion and infanticide. The time to stop both is now. As my administration acts to stop infanticide, we will be fully aware of the real issue that underlies the death of babies before and soon after birth.

Our society has, fortunately, become sensitive to the rights and special needs of the handicapped, but I am shocked that physical or mental handicaps of newborns are still used to justify their extinction. This administration has a Surgeon General, Dr. C. Everett Koop, who has done perhaps more than any other American for handicapped children, by pioneering surgical techniques to help them, by speaking out on the value of their lives, and by working with them in the context of loving families. You will not find his former patients advocating the so-called "quality-of-life" ethic.

I know that when the true issue of infanticide is placed before the American people, with all the facts openly aired, we will have no trouble deciding that a mentally or physically handicapped baby has the same intrinsic worth and right to life as the rest of us. As the New Jersey Supreme Court said two decades ago, in a decision upholding the sanctity of human life, "a child need not be perfect to have a worthwhile life."

Whether we are talking about pain suffered by unborn children, or about late-term abortions, or about infanticide, we inevitably focus on the humanity of the unborn child. Each of these issues is a potential rallying point for the sanctity of life ethic. Once we as a nation rally around any one of these issues to affirm the sanctity of life, we will see the importance of affirming this principle across the board.

Malcolm Muggeridge, the English writer, goes right to the heart of the matter: "Either life is always and in all circumstances sacred, or intrinsically of no account; it is inconceivable that it should be in some cases the one, and in some the other." The sanctity of innocent human life is a principle that Congress should proclaim at every opportunity.

It is possible that the Supreme Court itself may overturn its abortion rulings. We need only recall that in *Brown v. Board of Education* the court reversed its own earlier "separate but-equal" decision. I believe if the Supreme Court took another look at *Roe v. Wade,* and considered the real issue between the sanctity of life ethic and the quality of life ethic, it would change its mind once again.

As we continue to work to overturn *Roe v. Wade,* we must also continue to lay the groundwork for a society in which abortion is not the accepted answer to unwanted pregnancy. Pro-life people have already taken heroic steps, often at great personal sacrifice, to provide for unwed mothers. I recently spoke about a young pregnant woman named Victoria, who said, "In this society we save whales, we save timber wolves and bald eagles and Coke bottles. Yet, everyone wanted me to throw away my baby." She has been helped by Save-a-Life, a group in Dallas, which provides a way for unwed mothers to preserve the human life within them when they might otherwise be tempted to resort to abortion. I think also of House of His Creation in Coatesville, Pennsylvania, where a loving couple has taken in almost two hundred young women in the past ten years. They have seen, as a fact of life, that the girls are *not* better off having abortions than saving their babies. I am also reminded of the remarkable Rossow family of Ellington, Connecticut, who have opened their hearts and their home to nine handicapped adopted and foster children.

National Sanctity of Human Life Day, 1988

By the President of the United States of America

A Proclamation

America has given a great gift to the world, a gift that drew upon the accumulated wisdom derived from centuries of experiments in self-government, a gift that has irrevocably changed humanity's future. Our gift is twofold: the declaration, as a cardinal principle of all just law, of the God-given, unalienable rights possessed by every human being; and the example of our determination to secure those rights and to defend them against every challenge through the generations. Our declaration and defense of our rights have made us and kept us free and have sent a tide of hope and inspiration around the globe.

One of those unalienable rights, as the Declaration of Independence affirms so eloquently, is the right to life. In the 15 years since the Supreme Court's decision in *Roe v. Wade*, however, America's unborn have been denied their right to life. Among the tragic and unspeakable results in the past decade and a half have been the loss of life of 22 million infants before birth; the pressure and anguish of countless women and girls who are driven to abortion; and a cheapening of our respect for the human person and the sanctity of human life.

We are told that we may not interfere with abortion. We are told that we may not "impose our morality" on those who wish to allow or participate in the taking of the life of infants before birth; yet no one calls it "imposing morality" to prohibit the taking of life after people are born. We are told as well that there exists a "right" to end the lives of unborn children; yet no one can explain how such a right can exist in stark contradiction of each person's fundamental right to life.

That right to life belongs equally to babies in the womb, babies born handicapped, and the elderly or infirm. That we have killed the unborn for 15 years does not nullify this right, nor could any number of killings ever do so. The unalienable right to life is found not only in the Declaration of Independence but also in the Constitution that every President is sworn to preserve, protect, and defend. Both the Fifth and Fourteenth Amendments guarantee that no person shall be deprived of life without due process of law.

All medical and scientific evidence increasingly affirms that children before birth share all the basic attributes of human personality—that they in fact are persons. Modern medicine treats unborn children as patients. Yet, as the Supreme Court itself has noted, the decision in *Roe v. Wade* rested upon an earlier state of medical technology. The law of the land in 1988 should recognize all of the medical evidence.

Our Nation cannot continue down the path of abortion, so radically at odds with our history, our heritage, and our concepts of justice. This sacred legacy, and the well-being and the future of our country, demand that protection of the innocents must be guaranteed and that the personhood of the unborn be declared and defended throughout our land. In legislation introduced at my request in the First Session of the 100th Congress, I have asked the Legislative branch to declare the "humanity of the unborn child and the compelling interest of the several states to protect the life of each person before birth." This duty to declare on so fundamental a matter falls to the Executive as well. By this Proclamation I hereby do so.

NOW, THEREFORE, I, RONALD REAGAN, President of the United States of America, by virtue of the authority vested in me by the Constitution and laws of the United States, do hereby proclaim and declare the unalienable personhood of every American, from the moment of conception until natural death, and I do proclaim, ordain, and declare that I will take care that the Constitution and laws of the United States are faithfully executed for the protection of America's unborn children. Upon this act, sincerely believed to be an act of justice, warranted by the Constitution, I invoke the considerate judgment of mankind and the gracious favor of Almighty God. I also proclaim Sunday, January 17, 1988, as National Sanctity of Human Life Day. I call upon the citizens of this blessed land to gather on that day in their homes and places of worship to give thanks for the gift of life they enjoy and to reaffirm their commitment to the dignity of every human being and the sanctity of every human life.

IN WITNESS WHEREOF, I have hereunto set my hand this 14th day of January, in the year of our Lord nineteen hundred and eighty-eight, and of the Independence of the United States of America the two hundred and twelfth.

Ronald Reagan

The Adolescent Family Life Program, adopted by Congress at the request of Senator Jeremiah Denton, has opened new opportunities for unwed mothers to give their children life. We should not rest until our entire society echoes the tone of John Powell in the dedication of his book, *Abortion: The Silent Holocaust,* a dedication to every woman carrying an unwanted child: "Please believe that you are not alone. There are many of us that truly love you, who want to stand at your side, and help in any way we can." And we can echo the always-practical woman of faith, Mother Teresa, when she says, "If you don't want the little child, that unborn child, give him to me." We have so many families in America seeking to adopt children that the slogan "every child a wanted child" is now the emptiest of all reasons to tolerate abortion.

I have often said we need to join in prayer to bring protection to the unborn. Prayer and action are needed to uphold the sanctity of human life. I believe it will not be possible to accomplish our work, the work of saving lives, "without being a soul of prayer." The famous British member of Parliament William Wilberforce prayed with his small group of influential friends, the "Clapham Sect," for *decades* to see an end to slavery in the British empire. Wilberforce led that struggle in Parliament, unflaggingly, because he believed in the sanctity of human life. He saw the fulfillment of his impossible dream when Parliament outlawed slavery just before his death.

Let his faith and perseverance be our guide. We will never recognize the true value of our own lives until we affirm the value in the life of others, a value of which Malcolm Muggeridge says: "...however low it flickers or fiercely burns, it is still a Divine flame which no man dare presume to put out, be his motives ever so humane and enlightened."

Abraham Lincoln recognized that we could not survive as a free land when some men could decide that others were not fit to be free and should therefore be slaves. Likewise, we cannot survive as a free nation when some men decide that others are not fit to live and should be abandoned to abortion or infanticide. My administration is dedicated to the preservation of America as a free land, and there is no cause more important for preserving that freedom than affirming the transcendent right to life of all human beings, the right without which no other rights have any meaning.